Mortal Veins

Rhianna Levi

Dedication

This poetry book is for all those with mortal veins past, present, and future.

May your light always be brave and fierce.

Contents

Mortal Veins:

A beverage from mortal veins,

Serves well for humanity.

Pumped in marigold rays of kindness,

Coffee cups that play the game.

Those mortal veins,

Suffice to say,

Facilitate principal humanity;

Fineness.

Adroitness in relishing aerobicised emotion, an evocative

Marrow that God-like species moan for.

Those mortal veins peregrinate through the times,

Intact after passing,

Marigold lashings,

Bathing in their unfurled blossoms.

Sailing on our speckled skin pins and perishable fins.

How goodly it is that we cradle mortal veins.

Human-made tarmac:

Hearts have found intimacy with speedbumps birthed in tarmac -

Human-made.

Constructed with no easy fade.

Occasionally

Intentions find saliva beyond a person's mouth,

Closer to a spiritual black mass.

A bite, heavy on flesh and peeled nerves and growing bone.

Independent thought is kept. Stomping on with the struggle for plausible redemption,

The tearing of a blessing prayer.

No holy water was sought,

No small talk was said.

Fragrances of selfhood can be relocated when whistles are trained in symphonic melody with the rail track.

Blended with fever dreams echoed in the distortion of fairground mirrors.

The constructed loss of virginity occurs all over again—

In blatant reverse.

Hauntology Blessed In Poetry:

These passing prints whistle to past, present, future listeners.

In childlike handprints fastened to battled brick walls,

And adult writings of emotion scattered across building walls.

Hauntings bring us here,

Through the vessel maze of culture and politics,

They've remained here for forever after original and researched reflection.

We speak fear of things that wonder within our linguistics and passing thought.

Albeit, hauntology kindly permits us knowledge to discern,

Lighting better smoking log fires that make us better for future earth letters.

It's shadowed hauntings that reign as the most prized valiant asset in each story.

Their place is not in sketchy corners and backstreet alleyways.

Phases:

I measure intensity of my mental health in limbs shaking
at any one minute, and tears inhaled across my face.

Eye sockets and brunette body hair have become
acquainted in familiarity.

Deeply,

Uniquely,

Routinely.

Too many daggered degrees of heartbreak reside in this
youngster's chest cavity.

Amongst quivers,

Serotonin now pursues chaotic notions.

But oh, I love more thoroughly than most on the days I
feel fully me,

A bumblebee remarkably free.

I mind my mind in cheddar cheese moon phases,

But I won't change its charm or its planted gifts in
snowdrifts.

I finally accept its part in me.

This phenomenon is gratefully mine, and I did not have to pay a dime.

Requiem:

Long stood the rope swing that came to be.

Spectator of all,

In birth,

Maturity,

Inevitable dematerialisation in state.

It found a spot where beings muddled around its residency,

Taking a smug note of its persistence as each year came and went.

Until one day, the cunning insects found their way

With a bold snap,

Waving farewell to the playground equipment's reign.

The swing still plummeted in vain,

Believing an indestructible attitude would prevail above all;

Power would rule above any walls.

But placed on the scrap yard heap it now simmers in age,

Exposed to weather temperament and ventilation forged.

Conducting amazement that nothing remains anew,

And existence is a token not renewed.

It

    Eventually

        Sprinkles

          Quietly

            Away.

Futile relationship with hope:

Often searching overgrown leaves in desperation.

Ambition.

That living with weary sadness will be smoked into ash.

But of course our brains have become accustomed to battling overwhelming vastness.

Whisky glass and lethargic sleet

In fogged car windows that enlist null protection.

We have been here before - pinching at lead streamers coined in tin foil.

In an intention to be royalty.

It comes down to boiling all longing.

However even the darkest marshes have not given up on befriending brighter days.

There are always prospering dreams, shaped with divine fireflies,

doting childhood rhymes.

There is bliss to be found holding hands in solidarity.

Forever Fresh Acorns:

Dragged away by the neck scruff were the maple acorns
of the season,

With so much life to live beyond what was acceded,

Another inscription on an unduly and raw fresh stoned
flower bed instead.

Jolted to a halted cessation on Dover's sea whistled cliffs
in a manner that does not involve fists,

Teeth marks not so visible until Death has embarked on
its navigated trip.

Those men deserved kinder days,

Their lives should still be present in the day's respiratory
air.

The black dog is not fair,

No guilt or remorse to bare or share.

It's focus is to drive a full ship towards the new
destination,

No desire to help those men that were forcibly kept
close,

Or the families left in sight with no answered questions
or desired closure.

Across mystery of the rapture,

Keep their memory with you.

Soul Departed:

I wonder at times if the souls of the departed sing us
rainfall lullabies when clocks strike midnight.

Perhaps they are the reason that eventual comfort is felt
during prevalent times of need,

When we face dejected dreams which make us wish to
also be travelling alongside the faceless sea farer.

Towards the otherworldly.

Maybe they protect our items and possessions as we lay
in reflection on the dampened grass

And they urge us to respect times of grief and allow
ourselves to feel,
Regardless of the painfulness that we may initially feel.

I also wonder if those souls sit next to us on the
commute back home.

Full of golden opportunity to befriend identities not met
before.

Perhaps those departed souls wish for the same as us--to

feel a beating heartbeat once more.

Odyssey Knows It:

Odyssey spoke of power in the cryptic fingers of
midnight,
In the name of Circee,

Sweeping across lands once disbanded in Hallow's
catacomb eve.

Winter's figure comes reimagined in eclipses of fragrant
obscurity,
Numinous might progressed from sources in Alps that
uttered name days in

Bertha,

Befuna,

Perchta.

In likeness, lines traverse and bend in human's contortion
of spirit,
Sipping on fasting blood moons.

Majesty is of each witch,

Wiccan,

Pagan,

In between.

Expressing spells does not result in light writing itself
out of rolling stories.

It architects iced landscape trees,
Sheltering and bettering living marigold thyme.
For each misty home that arrives.

Lucifer Has Been Burnt By Flames Too:

Caffeine was drunk between eyelid memoirs and a somewhat passive Lucifer,

Under a conquered chestnut tree during the rawness of year's end.

A human lunged form cross legged on lost ground, Lucie meanwhile whistling to his own mental rhyme:

Flamed logs of a discarded campfire, just as heavy when Man and the downed angel first met.

That was the first time a bet was made between the two,

The bet deciphered that they could not,

Would not,

Should not

Experience heartbreak simultaneously.

That spoken bet disintegrated so very long ago.

Overthrown in the salmon coloured river a few feet away.

Now the minds of many hazard a guess,

That Lucie has a flame burnt heart too.

Allurement:

A calling of allure,
A waterside siren stalking each clasp,
As the storm absorbs a hypnotic solitude.

These swallowed faces in each wave
Are nothing that can be saved.
Their spirits have danced with each devil
Devoured each hydro level.

Vanished in the seabed, beyond these eroding rocks.
She is there each day, encompassing all devouring fame.

This sea is the greatest expedition.

Limbo:

A crumpled static
Held between the walls.

A flower of eloquence
Blooming through the door

A cracked window pane
With no option to remain definitively sane

Each and every day-
Maybe one day things will be the same.

Keys Are Of Importance:

There's a shrouded key.
It opens a treasure box.
Memories are held in that box which would rather be
forgotten.
Foolishly placed.
Launched into a ghoulish area,
Estimated to flood at approximately 04:17 hours into a
subjective design of the labelled future.

The future is perpetrated in the familiar territory of topic
lines of the interpretative past;
Slanted as a profile whose purpose is to drink blends of
lived happenings.
Slamming machinery across the floor at such speed.

Consequently kissing victims harshly,
As the typhoon plays rough pedestrian games in
multiverse realities,
A struggle in being appropriately understood in social
gathering rooms.

This is twinned with pains that everyone is constantly
avoiding and ignoring,
Then comes fickle dismay when thoughts collide in no
preparation or warning.

But those are moments that people need belief in,

Respecting the unfamiliarity of prodding strategies.

Jumping to attention with thrilling nanoseconds,
Skin cells respond in meeting surfaces and they fall to
sturdy ground.

Stroke skewers in the keys you've cupped.
As the storm takes a bleak exit- the key withholding
stories will stand.
Ignoring it makes it a little worse,
As haunted atoms is all that life breeds from:
Shake its vaporised hand with conviction.

Ribcage Is More:

Barbed wire and lily pollen wrap themselves in the bone
calcium of a youthful ribcage;
Tokened in respect for proceeding change.
Conditioned by firmness of sage.

Growing up was never safe.
Never comfortable in tribulations that pushed against
and into that young ribcage.

Where torment plays, so does a desire to go on and slay--
Healing the bruises lubricated on skin that has barely
seen a year,   nor originally
bargained to become known to a profusion of lit scars.

Sturdily, arm hairs fly tall whilst the ribcage refuses to
meet the floor.
And soft hands commit to the act of successfully
reaching the Edwardian's built door.

That is where the ribcage is no longer visible to meet
obstruction in groundwork.
Instead a youngster takes full reflective form,
Released in strength of knowledge and bone of trauma,
Befitting eventual joyfulness, fulfilment.

Truthful Afterlife:

There are words uttered,
Only in beat to autumn's divinity and serenity.

Creased leaves remain
on crimpled pages detailed on living and dying hearts.

When human eyes fade, the bliss of autumnal fall
remains.

Aiding hiking travellers on their journey—
through woods and shadowed mountains.

Arriving at the chestnut tree that bathes in harvest
rapturous harmony.
That is what is meant by contentment in eternity.

No thought jumps on command

Like Art, We Sail:

Perceptible acrylic paint nourishes all progressive states,
Like art, we sail to navigated new horizons:
Rings attached to our ankles, impersonating a personal
guide.
Meanings accelerate with each century:
We have the same entry, albeit differing streamlines.

Art Memoir:

On a bustling eve,

It was said,

That pianists marched on pavements from the day.

Sat down to tuck into a reaped feast with a table of leaves and

stories of imaginative heed.

Even Death found his table place and made a toast to those in company,

Yearning prosperous dealings with arts admired greatly from afar.

And then the critic himself took a shuddered leave. No

lives melodied away on that eve.

Conceivably,

Tastes of the expired remain artistic and brave.

Death has no dream to extract art away.

Musty Calling:

Palmed thistle hands,

Grasping at the musky underground.

Torched by drying lightning. Often viewed as a majestic

deity;

At dusk's beloved dark.

Specks of moisture between muddied toes,

Stretched walks in following

the woodland swamped calling,

They are the warning

His Decorum:

His detested fear of all in a cup,
With each rose scribed in blood idyllic ink.

He is just a transcendent skull on that dusty old shelf.

He will stare at you for hours- each smile is sour.
He is just waiting to devour.

He has dismissed his own cracks in blissful, deranged
ignorance.

His love is that perceptive, forgettable candle.
A cocoon of warm air with each developed flame.

He refrains from expressing a name, for that would just
drive him insane.

Devouring Aspirations:

Drowsy rings upon circulating veins-

    They hope to be downsized

with

    All venom.

Roasted with stretched saline skin, seeping through
distorted denim.

        End game.

I Never Did Find Out Where That Wheelbarrow Went:

I registered in time that hellos have greater meaning,
When fronted with **felt** goodbyes.

You never gave an understood **adieu.**

Instead,
Active participation in a vanishing dance took place.
Cryptic anonymous masks and all,
Impeccable in silencing a once followed scent.

Similar to the forestry green wheelbarrow I recall with
no second thought.
It ceased from **impression** in my childhood garden.
No knowledge of where it purposely sauntered its way
to.

That was countless years ago- it still **stings** so.

Permission, I Think Not:

Coil this fault in this head to fit elevation in drawn house
curtains of the revolving lease.

I do not see it,

But acknowledge my appetite to believe in it.

Whilst I hold my shaken stomach,

Rejecting nutrients my cells punch in arousal for.

Slurping desperately on what remains of me meanwhile.

Plucking eyelashes of the fainted images that I've
appealed to whilst in company of flaunted lions' dens.

Make me believe that I deserve to eat.

Gift space to be employed,

Not in view of pavement bins,

Falling to the curb in fountain downpours.

I think I need to eat,

But perhaps that is my fault- for requesting permission to
direct ardour to fleshed bones I occupy.

Occupy I shall,

Sexiness and wonder I will feel.

I will find the willingness to eat,

Rallying for my wellbeing,

Shaking my figurine on dancefloors,

No eyes will prey on mine.

One day my confidence will fully arrive,

But for now I need to ensure that I bring myself to finally eat.

Zip Lined Frenzy:

She tasted salted tears with the passing of frenzy.
Presumed to be away with devilish fairies whilst the
chaos of duelling world affairs sharpens in each
trembling boom.

He tasted salted tears with the passing of frenzy.
Unable to prevent the atrocities that his hippocampus
could not process;
Violence formed in thickness of bubble wrap.

They tasted salted tears with the passing of frenzy.
Loved ones ripped away from desperate arms of those
who cared,
Each heart becoming impaired with lightning striking far
more than twice.

You tasted salted tears with the passing of frenzy.
Too shaken to express what poison was injected into you
through vindictive actions spoken by serpents.
You evaluate yourself as a single sandal, floating in the
centre of the storm screaming in the medium of an
ocean.

We travel across zip lines, cautious of when the ungodly
'Snap' will burst interiors of eardrums and hearts.

Alarmed Recovery:

Nothing so silencing as a muzzled unseen alarm,
Indefatigable in its holler even when thought to have
been cut.

Recovery is the anxiety of a high street elevator
stumbling,
Reversing you back to sinking snow before.
10 steps forward,
5 more jumped back in the mind's active map.

I must not let it detract,
From ecstasy of cotton detergent in daylight's pearl-
Cinnamon of autumn's maple fete.
Recovery is the sister I never had,
The Father I miss the most,
Relighting my heart with fight like tonight's Sunday
roast.

I desire to amble creation's carpet far longer than first
thought.

A Case Of Day And Night:

Accustomed to the slithering silence,
That the night brings with each full vacating morality-
Fawned upon slit instability.
The oak trees dance, with each pivot clasping purpose.

A bat hunts for substance whilst a mellow rabbit dazes.
The leaves have made a pact with the absorbing green.

We hear the stories of nature's poweress,
Yet the experience is a
Gracious rarity in a knife's snake-like tongue.

Direct in assurance, the stars are a baby's comfort.
Gorging light in hypnosis of ephialtes.
Brazed in she wolf's bloodied lips of flesh on the soon to
be blotted,
Dessert will be the sourness of trudged rotten apples,
A similar treasure to poisoned arrows propelled in cusps
of skirmish.

It is believed that beyond a few hours, darkness bridges
to an end;
Ironic as bloodied howls are about to begin-

Throughout the siren stream of black dreams.

Know Yourself Best:

We speak our truths of today in hesitation that our voice
boxes will be scarred by judged indifference.
Looking at ourselves as concerning anomalies,
Flies that have found friction with a marbled spider web
floating mid air.

Pieces of a puzzle that appear unfitting of what is
expected upon conjugated play,
And unmanageable fretting on what should be or
should've been.
But at the final step, does any of that matter in finally
alleviating freely?

Cards have been communicated in speaking with
respected spell makers of the West,
But it must be remembered that we have the power to
fundamentally know ourselves best.
Even if our sinuses contest with congestion as we frame
our image as curious travellers,
Skating through iced lands.

Fast Lane:

Expressed in landscapes wide are slight addictions to
chilling with sad-slumped dandelions.

In the winter, and the spring,

Even rooms of love with people that kiss broken arts and
the sensitivity of hearts.

Moments cradled in lukewarm baths where artificial
bubbles bade farewell 30 minutes prior.

Chanting mottos of self belief. Hoping that with it
arrives bubble wrapped reassurance that mental illness is
not a dull sentence of grieved wreaths.

Lately, there have been no tears for some because salted
thoughts have dried them all up.

And people forget that tears are the elixir of all our
hectic lives;

They aid in processing the bad, and remembering why
each of us are alive—defying any illness because our
souls and bonds are so magnificently bold.

Observe comfort in the laws of gravity that keep your
cool pose on earth's ground and the magnitude of atoms
flowing in your physical.

Take flight on the fast lane.

Do not ignore the fluidity of emotions;

Sometimes it is necessary to experience uncomfortable stones in shoe wear on the grained path,

Eventually reaching higher ground that blissfully dreams across sea and sandy land.

Simple acts can be the reminder of the undeniable validity of our living, breathing being.

Turn the kettle on, at times a philosophical meeting with a cup of tea is incontestably needed.

We all need welcoming doors in our gaze when sunlight at times stray.

Blissful, Fragmented Wildness:

Wildness springs to calm minds stuck in motion on
gravel ground,

Find moments to awaken feral temperaments that need

Appreciation,

Positioning,

Marking.

Swimming to beats that make more than human skin
dance:

Bare foot blood tapping through to undergrowth shoots.

This could not be achieved in a moment of wearing steel
boots.

Wildness is a feral love that holds the hands of lovers
and connected friends.

Why deny what is a lifelong thirst?

Rosé Person:

There's a splinter in my toe that stubbornly refuses to go,

As I sink into wooden flooring absorbed into a unwitnessed abode.

Gazed upon by a growling crow that sweats from its feathered gown onto my unsuspecting brow.

Is this how we grow?

Pushing ourselves sideways into toxicity to compactly perfect the shapes accepted in this world.

It's not right and alas

I am so tired.

I have no intention of wanting perfection.

See me as a bloodied glass of rose wine:

Sweet and sour:

Magnifying electric emotion.

Showering in specks of rain water that drip drops from seeping and constructed ceilings.

I am not perfection, but I am infatuated with this rose permed evolution.

We Wish For Sandpits Everywhere:

Grains of sand swallowed my feet in the communal sand
pit during childhood- they still do.

Blanketing each toe with joy- contentment.

Attempts to count individual grains lacked success but
oh I kept trying.

A child's mind equates this pit to an opportunity to build
things that were once destroyed in quick succession.

No constraints in building a castle;

No need to source money or resources to build
something anew.

Imagination leads the way.

Sandpits create single moments of fulfilment for us all.

I somewhat admit to wanting to be made of it;
indestructible (Somewhat remarkable).

Speak For Those No Longer Here:

When is it justified to
                    Shoot one's heart with a spiteful
gun.

To disallow insurgency, revolt for those voices of
            Children
                    Spirits
                        Aspiring adults

Whose demise was sorted after in something that was
beyond good human
                        Contrive.
Justice is not best served cold,
But through a warm mind and passion articulated in the
word:

            CEASE.

Printed in Poland
by Amazon Fulfillment
Poland Sp. z o.o., Wrocław